# The 'ot' Plot
# VI

By Viola & Zaida Stefano

**VeeZee Publications**

Copyright © VeeZee Publications Pty. Ltd. 2024
First published in Australia in 2024
by VeeZee Publications Pty. Ltd.
veezeepublications.com

The right of Viola Stefano to be identified as the author of this work have been asserted by her in accordance with the **Copyright Amendment (Moral Rights) Act 2000.**

All rights reserved. Apart from any use as permitted by the author & under the **Copyright Act 1968**, no part may be reproduced, copied, scanned, stored in a retrieval system, recorded, or shared, by any means or in any form, without prior written & signed authorization from the publisher.

ISBN: 978-1-923120-15-0

A catalogue record of this book is available from the **National Library of Australia.**

Author: Viola Stefano
Illustrations, cover & internal designs: Zaida Stefano

Illustrations copyright © Zaida Stefano 2024
Design copyright © Zaida Stefano 2024

**Disclaimer:** The content presented in this book is meant for educational purposes only. The author & publisher claim no accountability to any entity or person for any liability, damage, or loss caused or assumed to be caused directly or indirectly as a consequence of the application, use, or interpretation of the material in this book.

# Core words used in this book

| I | want | can | stop | look |
|---|---|---|---|---|
| like | more | he | go | see |
| here | what | do | the | and |
| out | where | we | it | up |
| not | they | when | that | down |
| she | now | them | is | put |
| help | off | you | yes | on |
| turn | who | this | no | why |
| done | make | a | to | under |
| come | in | some | which | there |
| open | get | good | same | home |

The big gorilla lives

on a plot.

In this spot over here,

that is very hot.

He sits on a log and can see a lot of dots.

The dots look like spots.

I don't know any hogs with spots or dogs with dots.

That is not a hog or a dog.

What animal with spots and dots is on the trot?

It will not stop for the gorilla to see.

The gorilla hops down from the log and turns to look.

He does not see spots and dots. The animal is gone.

It will not come back

for the gorilla to see.

# Words with 'ot' in this book

| plot | trot | spot |
|---|---|---|
| not | hot | dots |
| spots | lot | |

## Words with a short 'o' sound in this book

| hog | stop | dog |
|---|---|---|
| hops | log | gone |
| on | from | hogs |
|  | dogs |  |

# Learning made easy with VeeZee

**VeeZee Publications**

## Wait, there's more!

Visit our website for information about our range of readers & supporting products.

**veezeepublications.com**

www.ingramcontent.com/pod-product-compliance
Lightning Source LLC
Chambersburg PA
CBHW042107090526
44590CB00004B/126